MATERIALS:
Old Game Pieces paper
• Cutable strips: Typewriter, Print Blocks, Letter Squares • Black wire clip • Watch crystal • 6 BBs • 2½" x 3½" chipboard card • Matboard • *Tsukineko* Pinecone Versacolor cube • Japanese screw punch • 2.0 punch bit • Hypo-Tube Cement • PVA glue

INSTRUCTIONS:
Adhere Game Pieces paper to chipboard card. Adhere to matboard. Ink card edges with Pinecone. • Punch 6 small holes in the 'Mello's Dairy' circle. Drop 6 BBs into the holes. Line the rim of a watch crystal with Hypo-Tube Cement and set it down on the circle. Let dry. • Cut out 'Fun & Games' and bingo pieces. Age with Pinecone ink. Glue to card. • Attach clip.

Fun and Games
Remember those games you used to have as a kid where you had to get all the balls into the little holes? Here's a mini version you can make. To find ball bearings this tiny, you'll have to buy inexpensive party favors and tear them apart.

By the Sea
Preserve sand and tiny shells in a watch crystal shaker. Shakers are a great embellishment.

MATERIALS:
At the Beach paper • Seaside Milestones stickers • White metal clip • 2½" x 3½" chipboard card • 2 watch crystals • Sand • Seashells • Seashell charm and holder • *Hero Arts* Playful alphabet stamps • *Tsukineko* inks (Pansy Impress, Hyacinth Versacolor cube) • Hypo-Tube Cement • Glue stick

INSTRUCTIONS:
Glue Beach paper to chipboard card. Ink card edge with Hyacinth. • Affix sticker to back of card. Trim. • Fill a watch crystal with sand. Apply cement to crystal edge. Set card over crystal. Press gently to adhere. • Fill the other crystal with small shells. Adhere to card. • Affix shell charm with charm holder. • Stamp 'By the Sea' using Pansy ink. • Attach clip.

It's About Time
Time flies when you're having fun. I hope you enjoy making this timely shaker card.

MATERIALS:
Tea Dye Clocks paper • Cutable strips: Letter Square, Print Blocks, Toy Blocks, Dark Words, Typewriter • Mail Art Backs Trading Card • Rulers cardstock • Watch crystal • Watch parts • 2 Copper eyelets • *Tsukineko* Bark Versacolor cube • *Sizzix* watch hands die cut • Hypo-Tube Cement • Foam tape • Glue stick

INSTRUCTIONS:
Cut Artist Trading Card from Mail Art Backs. Round corners. Glue Clocks paper to back. Ink card edge. • Die cut watch hands from Rulers cardstock. Glue to card. Set eyelets. • Cut out letters, ink edges Glue to card. • Tape watch face in place. • Fill crystal. Apply cement to edge of crystal.

Shaker Bubble Cards

Hypo-Tube Cement is indispensable for adhering shaker bubbles.

In addition to being a very strong glue, it has a hypodermic needle applicator which allows you to apply glue to the very thin edge of the crystal.

Adhering a Watch Crystal to a Card

Put items inside crystal. Apply Hypo-Tube Cement to watch crystal edge.

Your creative time will be more productive if you have a few things at your fingertips for easy access. These items are basic to my art. I'm sure you have your own favorites.

Adhesives: The purple UHU glue stick glides on smoothly and the color lets you see where you've applied it. It dries clear. UHU sticks paper to paper or cardstock, but it won't bear any weight. For items that must bend, PVA glue is good. When you have something heavy, you can't beat Glue Dots. Remember to apply these directly from the paper to your work because they will stick to your fingers as fiercely as they stick to your art. 3M foam mounting tape is also a staple adhesive.

Inks: I prefer Tsukineko inks. For aging and edging, I use Bark and Pinecone Versacolor cubes for everything. I almost never leave edges bare. It takes a little extra time but it gives the piece a finished look. The other ink I use is StazOn. As a solvent based ink, it dries on any surface – paper, wood, metal, plastic. The re-inkers are great for aging metal pieces like shiny charms. If you don't want to buy different inks for different applications, StazOn is a good choice and it comes in a variety of colors.

Tools: These are the tools you'll want to have handy:

• A sharp craft knife with snap-off blades. Accidents happen when your blade is dull. These blades are inexpensive and literally a snap to replace.

• A cutting mat protects your workplace. A newsprint pad is useful for applying glue or paint. When a page gets messy, just tear it off and throw it away.

• A bone folder or other dull edge for scoring.

• Scissors with a Teflon edge for cutting sticky papers.

• A *Fiskars* 12" paper cutter saves time cutting paper and cardstock to size without the need to measure.

• An *Olfa* 6" x 12" quilting ruler allows you to measure and cut with precision.

Trading Card Swap Book

Here's another spectacular way to show off your cards. I used neutral tones so the book would not clash with the art inside. Rub-ons are an easy way to decorate the cover. Notice the date and place of the swap on the closure ribbons.

MATERIALS:
10 sheets Rulers cardstock • 2 matboards 3⅝" x 4½" • 2 pieces Tan cover paper 5⅝" x 6½" • 6 sheets 12" x 12" Deep Tan cardstock • 1½ yards Brown waxed linen thread • 2 feet Brown ribbon • Rub-ons for cover title and ribbon detail • 14 ATCs for inserts • *Tsukineko* Bark Versacolor cube • Needles • PVA glue • Double-sided tape • Glue stick

INSTRUCTIONS:
Hole punching template: Copy the spine hole pattern onto stiff cardstock and cut it out. Score on the center line.

Preparing the signatures: **Layer 1:** Cut 7 Deep Tan cardstocks 3⅝" x 9". Fold each piece to 3⅝" x 4½". • **Layer 2:** Cut 7 Rulers cardstocks 3" x 7¼". Fold each piece to 3" x 3⅝". Now fold each sheet in half again to 3⅝" x 1½". Note: The long fold will now measure 3⅝", the same height as the first layer.

Punching holes: Nest Layer 2 inside Layer 1 with folded end of Layer 2 at bottom. • Nest template inside layers. Punch 4 holes following the template. Repeat for all signatures. We will refer to the two middle holes as 'center holes' and the first and last holes as the 'end holes'.

Sewing: Thread a needle on each end of the waxed linen. Beginning inside the first signature, push the needles through the two center holes to the outside of the spine so that the midpoint of the thread is between the two center holes. Cross the needles and thread back through the center holes to the inside of the signature. *With each needle, go directly out the nearest end hole to the outside of the signature. • Add the 2nd signature next to the first, taking care to match the open ends of Layer 2. Push each needle into the corresponding end hole of the 2nd signature. Pull the threads snugly to tighten but not so tightly as to tear the cardstock. Now push each needle through the nearest center hole of the 2nd signature and pull to the outside of the spine. Cross the threads and insert each needle into the center holes, pulling the thread to the inside. Add signatures and repeat from * until all 7 signatures have been sewn. When the sewing is finished, tie off the threads with a square knot.

Assembling the book: Notice when you close the book, two pieces of Deep Tan cardstock are back to back in six places. Glue these layers together where they meet. Be careful not to get glue anywhere but these sheets. Place the book block under a heavy weight and set aside to dry.

Covers: Cover the matboards with cover paper. Miter the corners. Cut the ribbon in half. On the short side of each cover, securely tape a ribbon to the inside. • Adhere the covers to the book block with PVA, making sure that the ribbons are on the open side of the book and not the spine side. Align the covers and replace the weight. Let dry.

Layer 3: Cut 7 Deep Tan cardstocks 3⅝" x 6½". Fold to 3⅝" x 3¼". • Apply PVA glue to outside edges of each 3⅝" side and insert it into one of the open signatures. Make sure that you glue just the edges of the insert to the edges of the signature. This forms the star. • Repeat for the other 6 signatures. • Put under heavy weight. Let dry.

Layer 4: Cut 7 Rulers cardstocks 5½" x 7¼". Fold to 2¾" x 7¼". Open and fold to 3⅝" x 5½". Open. Refold to 2¾" x 7¼". Draw and cut diagonal following the diagram on page 5. Re-fold to form two pockets. • Apply PVA glue to outside edges of each 3⅝" side of a folded pocket. Insert into an open signature. Make sure that you glue just the edges of the insert to the edges of the signature. This forms the ATC pockets. • Repeat for the other 6 signatures. • Put under heavy weight. Let dry.

Finish: Insert ATC cards into the pockets. Decorate the cover as desired.

Making a Star Book

1. Punch holes in signatures.

2. Sew signatures with waxed linen thread.

3. Glue Layer 3 in place with glue stick.

4. Glue pocket layer in place with PVA glue.

5. Add ATCs in pockets.

Star Book for Trading Cards

LAYER 4 DIAGRAM

PUNCH SPINE HOLES

Cut line

SIGNATURE PAGE PATTERN

Fold

SPINE PATTERN
MAKE 7
Fold spine in half horizontaly and
fold again vertically.
Punch holes after piece is folded.

Fold

Fold

ATC Swap Ideas

While you're sitting in your studio, waiting for someone to ask you to join an ATC swap, why not host one of your own? Here are a few ideas of swaps to start:

Four Seasons • Alphabetica • Favorite Quotes • Children

Animals/Pets • Food • Travel – My favorite City/Country
Politics or political figures • Book Club • Films
Pick a favorite artist, musician, historical figure, author
Pick a decade – The Roaring 20s, the 60s
Color swap – For example, everyone work in Red
Pick a category from this book:

Moving Parts, Cards that Open, Miniature books

Shaker Cards... continued from pages 2 - 3

Artist Trinkets

Matboard is the secret to making this card thick enough to support the watch crystals.

MATERIALS:
Toy Blocks cardstock • Color Words Cutable strip • 2½" x 3½" chipboard card • Matboard • 2 watch crystals • Assorted beads • *Tsukineko* Versacolor cubes (Bark, Green Tea) • Craft knife • Hypo-Tube Cement • PVA glue • Glue stick

INSTRUCTIONS:
Fill one watch crystal half full of beads. Apply cement to the rim of the crystal. Adhere second crystal to the first. Let dry. • Glue Toy Blocks cardstock to chipboard card. Trim. • Glue chipboard card to matboard with PVA. Trim. Ink card edges with Bark. • Lay a crystal on the card. Trace the outline. Cut slightly inside the tracing. The double crystal should just fit inside the cut-out. If needed, trim to fit. Do not cut too much away or the crystal will slip out. • Apply cement to the hole in the cardstock. Insert the crystal. Let dry. • Cut out words. Ink edges with Green Tea. Adhere to card with PVA glue.

Adhering a Watch Crystal to a Card

Put items inside crystal. Apply Hypo-Tube Cement to watch crystal edge.

Blue Eyed Beauty

Laminate tile samples are great to use when you're treating your base with wet applications because there is no buckling or curling. You can drill holes with a Dremel tool if you want to dangle charms. Eyelets are not needed since tiles won't tear.

MATERIALS:
Dictionary paper • Cutable strips: Typewriter, Print Blocks • Kraft cardstock • 2½" x 3½" chipboard card • Laminate tile • Blue rhinestone • 2 Brass corner pieces • Brass jump ring • Heart charm • Alpha-cap • Rubber stamps (*Ornamentum* Lady's face; *Stampa Rosa* writing background) • *Ranger* Latte Adirondack alcohol ink • *Tsukineko* inks (Black StazOn; Bark Versacolor cube) • Copper Topper paint • Green Patina • Prismacolor colored pencils (Flesh, Red) • *Dremel* drill • Drill bit • Foam tape • Glue dots • Glue stick

INSTRUCTIONS:
Cover chipboard card with Dictionary paper. Edge with Bark ink. • Cut out rulers, pencils and "Journey" letters. Edge pieces in Bark ink. Adhere to card. • Age bottle cap with Latte ink. Cut watch face from Typewriter strip. Glue to bottle cap with PVA. • Paint laminate chip with 2 coats of Copper. When the second coat is tacky, brush with patina. Let dry. • Stamp tile with Black ink. • Stamp face in Black ink on Kraft cardstock. Trim and shade with colored pencils. Glue to tile with PVA. • Drill a small hole in the bottom right of tile. Attach heart charm with jump ring. • Adhere Brass corners and bottle cap clock with glue dots. Glue rhinestone with PVA. Adhere tile to card with foam tape.

My Girl

ATC's are the perfect size for showing off your small photos.

MATERIALS:
Rulers cardstock • Cutable strips: Typewriter, Print Blocks • Puzzle pieces • 2½" x 3½" chipboard card• *Tsukineko* Versacolor cubes (Bark, Pinecone) • PVA glue • Glue dots • Glue stick

INSTRUCTIONS:
Adhere photo to chipboard card. • Cut out 4 rulers, 2 pencils and "My Girl" letters. • Overlap ruler ends to fit card. Miter corners. Ink ruler edges with Bark. Curl rulers slightly so that the center of the frame opens outward. Apply PVA to the outside edges of rulers and adhere in place. • Edge letters with Pinecone ink. Adhere to frame with PVA glue. • Edge pencils with Bark ink and adhere to frame with PVA glue. Adhere puzzle pieces to frame corners with glue dots.

Treating a Laminate Tile with Copper Patina

1. Apply 2 coats of Copper Topper paint to tile.

2. When second coat is tacky, dab Patina Green on tile. Let dry.

3. Stamp tile with Black StazOn ink.

4. Decorate as desired.

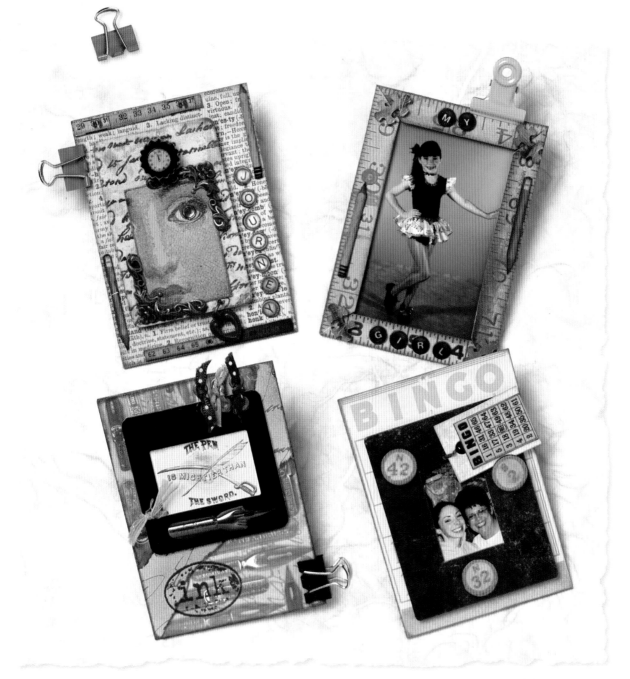

Ink

The art of writing has changed dramatically over the centuries. This themed ATC recalls a time of beautiful handwriting and nib tip pens.

MATERIALS:

Journaling cardstock • Black slide mount • Black wire clip • Writing Background paper • 2½" x 3½" chipboard card • 6 Brass eyelets • 3 ribbons • 2" Gold fiber • Ephemera image • Fountain pen tip • *Stamp in the Hand* Ink stamp • *Ranger* Caramel Adirondack ink • *Tsukineko* inks (Black StazOn; Bark Versacolor cube) • Stipple brush • PVA glue • Dimensional glue dots • Glue stick

INSTRUCTIONS:

Cover chipboard card with Writing Background paper. Stipple with Caramel ink. • Tear Journaling cardstock, edge with Bark ink and glue in place. Edge card with Bark ink. • Stamp "ink" in Black in bottom left corner. • Set 3 Brass eyelets in top right of card and slide mount. Adhere ephemera image to mount with glue stick. • Punch a small hole in mounted image. Thread Gold fiber and tie a knot. Adhere slide mount to card. Thread ribbons through pairs of eyelet holes and knot. • Adhere pen tip with glue dots. • Cover card back as desired. Attach wire clip.

Frames for Photos on Trading Cards

Whether showing off your kids' pictures or your own creation, all fine art should have a frame. Here are some simple ideas to get you started.

Bingo

It's time for fun and games. The dangling Bingo card hides a photo.

MATERIALS:

Bingo paper • Print Blocks Cutable strip • Vintage slide mount • Red fiber • 2½" x 3½" chipboard card • *Tsukineko* Versacolor cubes (Bark, Pinecone) • Foam tape • Glue stick

INSTRUCTIONS:

Cover chipboard card with Bingo paper. Edge with Bark ink. • Glue photo to mount. Edge mount in Pinecone ink. Punch a hole in the top center portion of mount. • Cut out Bingo card and playing pieces. Edge with Bark ink. Adhere Bingo card to Cream tag and tie to mount with Red fiber. • Tape playing pieces and mount to card.

ATC's with Moving Parts

Watch hands that revolve, charms that dangle, propellers that spin, pieces that slide in and out – all these cards have moving parts to keep your interest.

Timeless Treasure

Make a Timeless Treasure in no time at all.

MATERIALS:
Small metal disk • Tea Dye Clocks paper • Cardstock: Rulers, Time • Dark Words Cutable strips • White wire clip • Watch Hands punch • Brown brad • Altered alphabet letter T • "Treasure" rub-on • *Ranger* Latte Adirondack alcohol ink • *Tsukineko* Bark Versacolor color cube • Sanding block • Double-sided foam tape • Glue stick

INSTRUCTIONS:
Cut the Brown word card from the cutable strip so it is 2½" x 3½". Round corners. Trace onto Tea Dye Clocks paper and cut out. • Glue Brown card to Clocks paper. Ink edges with Bark. Sand both sides. • Apply Latte ink directly to disk edges and air dry. • Cut clock face from Time cardstock. Ink with Bark. • Punch watch hands from Rulers cardstock. Ink with Bark. • Affix hands to clock face loosely with brad. • Use foam tape to affix clock face to disk and disk to card. • Cut out T Altered Alphabet and ink with Bark. Glue to bottom left of card. • Add rub-on word to complete the word "Treasure".

1. Apply Latte alcohol ink directly to metal disk.

2. Cut out watch face from Time cardstock and age.

3. Punch clock hands from Rulers cardstock and age.

4. Attach hands to clock face loosely with brad.

5. Attach clock face to metal disk with foam tape.

Little Boy Blue

The sky's the limit when using aviation themes. The dangling plane and spinning propeller charms capture the eye with movement.

MATERIALS: Blue A-Z Word Blocks paper • Cutable strips: Letter Squares, Print Blocks, Typewriter, Wings and Things • 2½" x 3½" chipboard card • Charm hanger • Propeller • Airplane charm • *Tsukineko* ink (Cornflower walnut; Versacolor cubes: Bark, Pinecone) • Sanding block • PVA glue • Foam tape • Glue stick

INSTRUCTIONS: Glue chipboard card to A-Z paper. Trim. Ink card edges with Bark. • Dab walnut ink on card border with a paper towel. Sand. • Punch or cut out elements. Age "little" with Pinecone ink. Ink all other elements with Bark. • Affix all pieces with PVA. • Attach propeller charm with foam tape. Attach airplane charm with a charm hanger.

Executive Decision Maker

Use this card for all important decisions.

MATERIALS: Target paper • 2⅜" spinner • Brass brad • Red metal clip • 2½" x 3½" chipboard card • Matboard • *Hero Arts* Printer's Type alphabet stamps • *Tsukineko* ink (Silver Encore, Pinecone Versacolor cube) • PVA glue

INSTRUCTIONS: Lay spinner on top of chipboard card so that the hole is centered. Mark and punch hole. • Lay chipboard card over Target paper so the hole is over the center of the target. Trace card, cut out, glue to chipboard and punch hole. • Glue card to matboard. Trim, punch center hole and ink edges with Pinecone. Stamp yes, no and maybe in Silver ink. Attach spinner to card with brad. Attach clip to card.

Introductions with Style
by Leslie McFarlane and Mary Kaye Seckler

What artist could ask for a better introduction? And it's fast and easy to make too!

MATERIALS:
Mail Art Backs Trading Card • Pink metal clip • Cardstock: Gumballs, Jade Pattern, Blithe • Coin envelope template • *Tsukineko* Versacolor cubes (Atlantic, Bark) • ¾" circle punch • PVA glue • Glue stick

INSTRUCTIONS: Trace Mail Art Card back onto Blithe cardstock. Cut out and adhere with glue stick to card back. Ink edges with Atlantic. • Make envelope with Gumballs cardstock using PVA. • Cut off envelope top. Punch a ¾" half circle in the envelope end. Ink edges with Bark. • Cut a strip of Jade Pattern cardstock. Age with Bark ink and wrap around envelope. Glue in place. • Glue envelope to card back. • Punch two ¾" holes from Blithe cardstock and glue back-to-back to top of business card. Insert card into holder. • Add clip.

Journey Sliders... Green and Red

This slider card has a green front and a red back because the Salsa mount comes that way. I love to take advantage of dual-sided mounts and cardstocks when I create two-sided art!

MATERIALS:
Exotic Lands Trading Card • Light Words Cutable strip • Salsa slide mount • Blue metal clip • *Tsukineko* inks (Black StazOn; Versacolor cubes: Evergreen, Rose Red, Bark) • Rubber stamps (*Tin Can Mail* small writing; *Hero Arts* Kanji Poem) • Chipboard 2⅛" x 2⅞" • Sanding block • Foam tape • PVA glue • Glue stick

INSTRUCTIONS:
Holder: Close mount and trim 1" off the side that opens. • Put ¼" wide pieces of foam tape on the outer edge of the inside seam, and sides of mount. Remove paper backing from foam tape and close mount. • Sand both sides. Ink the Red side with Rose Red and the Green side with Evergreen. Stamp small writing stamp on mount with Black ink. • **Slide-Out**: Green side: Cut image from Exotic Lands strip. Glue to chipboard. Trim. Cut out 'journey' word. Ink edges with Bark. Glue in place with PVA. Stamp Kanji poem on left side of image with Black ink. • Red side: Adhere ephemera image to back of chipboard. Ink slide-out edges with Bark. Slide into holder.

Making a Slider Card

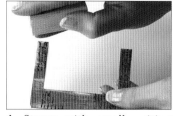

1. Close slide mount and trim 1" off edge opposite fold.

2. Adhere foam tape strips on inside fold, top and bottom of mount edges.

3. Distress with sanding block and age with Rose Red and Evergreen inks.

4. Stamp with small writing stamp using Black ink.

Miniature Books

I'm a book artist, so I'm always looking for ways to fit books into art. These books are simple enough to make for a limited swap but you might not want to try them for a large-scale swap. Remember, you can always make just one for yourself.

Love Notes

I am very practical so this Post-it-note holder appeals to me. If it's too thick for your tastes, just peel half of the notes off before adhering them to the cover.

MATERIALS: Handmade Backs Trading Card • Traveler cardstock • Chipboard cover: Two 2" x 2½", One ¼" x 2½" • Cover paper: One 3½" x 5¾" • Liner paper: One 2¼" x 4¼" • Life's Journey Stamp Collage paper • Brass eyelet • Elastic tie • Pink Post-it-note pad • *Hero Arts* Printer's Type alphabet stamps • *Tsukineko* inks (Old Rose Impress; Versacolor cubes: Bark, Vanilla) • Foam tape • Glue stick

INSTRUCTIONS: **Card:** Cut out Artist Trading card. Cover with cardstock with Rose side facing out. Age edges with Bark ink. Stamp Love Notes on top of Rose side in Old Rose ink. • **Book:** Adhere chipboard cover pieces to cover paper according to the diagram. • Fold cover paper toward the chipboard. Miter corners. Glue in place. • Glue liner papers to the inside to hide the chipboard. • **Pages:** Peel the backing off the Post It Notes and adhere to inside of book. • **Cover:** Cut out image to decorate cover. Ink edges with Vanilla. Adhere to cover with glue stick. • **Closure:** Punch a hole and set an eyelet on the right side of the back cover. Insert elastic tie ends through the hole and wrap around book to secure. Add foam tape to the back cover and adhere book to card. To open note cover, just wrap the elastic cord around the back of the card.

Making a Post-it-Note-Cover

1. Miter corners. Wrap and glue flaps.

2. Glue liner paper to inside.

3. Decorate as desired.

4. Insert cord ends through eyelet hole in back.

Musical Notes

The best part of this ATC is the closure that doubles as a pencil holder for a tiny pencil.

MATERIALS: Cutable strips: Typewriter, Dark Words, Toy Blocks • Cardstock: Library, Journaling • 2½" x 3½" chipboard card • Tiny pencil • Yellow text paper • 2 musical note charms • Black/Gold metallic thread • Needle • Sanding block • ¼" wide red liner tape • Glue stick • PVA glue

INSTRUCTIONS: **Card:** Cover chipboard card with Journaling cardstock. Distress slightly with sanding block. • **Book:** Cut out music and government books from Library cardstock in one piece. Fold in half vertically. Round corners of folded cover. • Cut out 2 pieces of Yellow paper slightly smaller than the open cover. Fold those pages and nest them one inside the other and nest inside cover. Make 3 holes in the spine and sew a three-hole pamphlet stitch in the book using Black/Gold thread. • **Pamphlet stitch:** Begin on the outside of the book at the top hole and insert needle. Draw thread through and exit the center hole. Re-enter the bottom hole and exit the center hole again. Tie off thread with a square knot at the top hole. • Attach music note charms to the thread ends. • **Pencil closure:** Cut 2 pieces from Journaling cardstock ¼" x 2¼". Wrap a strip around the pencil. Adhere strip ends together so the pencil fits tightly. Adhere strip ends to the inside of the back of the book. Repeat for front cover, laying the strip just above the back cover strip. Close book and insert pencil to close. • Glue book to card with PVA. Decorate pages of book as desired.

Making a Pencil Closure

 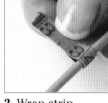  

1. Cut 2 strips of cardstock.

2. Wrap strip around pencil.

3. Adhere strip ends together and adhere to cover.

4. Thread pencil through both closures.

Cut away corners as shown

1/4"
2"   2"
2-1/2"   2-1/2"
3-1/2"
5-3/4"

Making a Piano Hinge Book

  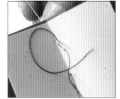

. Curve spine
round skewer.

2. Thread skewer
through hinge.

3. Sew signatures
into valley folds of
rust card.

Piano Hinge Tag Book
by Melissa David and Mary Kaye Seckler

I first saw this little tag book many years ago in a wonderful stamp store in Iowa. This proves that reat art gets around because the creator, Melissa David, is from Texas.

MATERIALS: Toy Blocks cardstock • 2½" x 3½" chipboard card • 1 thick amboo skewer • Rust cardstock 3" x 5" • 6 Balsa text papers 2⅞" x 3½" 2 glass beads • Large Gold brad • Elastic tie • Gold pen • 18" Bronze metalic thread • Rubber stamps (*Limited Edition* London Gentleman; *Just for Fun* lock face; *Penny Black* Letter background) • *Tsukineko* inks (Rusty Brown tazOn, Bark Versacolor cube) • Matte Mod-Podge • Needle • Bone folder PVA glue • Foam tape • Glue stick

INSTRUCTIONS: Card: Glue chipboard card to Toy Blocks cardstock and rim. • **Book:** Trace Piano Hinge pattern onto Toy Blocks cardstock and cut ut. Stamp Green side of front cover using Rusty Brown ink. Coat both sides f cover with several thin layers of Mod-Podge, drying between coats. • dge front cover and spine squares with Gold pen. • Shape center part etween the two rows of squares by placing a skewer on the Green side and olling the cover gently around it. Repeat the procedure by placing the skewr on the blocks side of the cover along each row of squares. Doing this will tart the spine curving in the proper direction. • Thread the skewer from the ottom of the cover, pointed end first, into the hinge that the rows of quares form when nested into each other. Pull the ends of the covers genly to show the woven spine. • Flatten the narrow piece of cardstock that rotrudes beyond the skewer on the inside of the cover. Remove the skewr and apply small dots of PVA glue to the inside of the hinge. Re-insert the kewer so that the point extends about a half inch beyond the top of the ook. Trim off the end of the skewer. Add glass beads to the point of the kewer. • **Rust cardstock:** Fold cardstock 2½" x 3". Lay the mountain fold ver the inside of the spine and press the cardstock down over the skewer. Remove the cardstock and flatten the two new folds with a bone folder. Now ou should have a W-shaped piece of cardstock.

HINGE PATTERN FOR TOY BLOCK CARDSTOCK

(dotted line is horizontal center)

• **Signatures:** Fold Text papers to 1¾" x 2⅞". Nest into 2 signatures (groups of pages) of 3 pages each. • Nest one signature inside the first valley fold, punch three holes in the signature and rust card. Sew the signature into the card using a three-hole pamphlet stitch. • **Pamphlet stitch:** Start on the inside in the center hole. Insert the needle and exit the signature. Re-enter the signature in the top hole, exit the signature at the bottom hole. Re-enter at the center hole and tie off with a square knot. Repeat for the other signature. • **Join Signatures to Book:** Apply PVA glue on the outside of the Rust cardstock in the space between the two signatures. Adhere the Rust cardstock over the small strip of Toy Blocks cardstock on the inside of the cover. • **Closure:** Insert the brad at the center right side of the front cover. Punch a hole in the card at the right side and thread the elastic tie through from the finished side. Wrap the elastic around the side of the card and over the brad for a closure.

ATC's that Open

Think of all the things you could hide in an envelope or file folder. My favorite is the standing photo frame that opens to reveal someone special. You might put it on your desk at work and close it up and take it home with you.

Live, Laugh, Love

Make files with photos of all your secret pals. These cards are great for sharing and swapping.

MATERIALS:
Handmade Backs Trading Cards • Cutable strips: Dark Words, Light Words • Mini file folders: large Black, medium Red, small Khaki • Red paper • 2½" x 3½" chipboard card • 3 photos • Black elastic closure • Brass photo swivel • Brass brad • 2 Brass eyelets • *Invoke Art* Heart stamp • *Ranger* (Perfect Bronze Perfect Pearls, Perfect Medium) • *Tsukineko* Versacolor cubes (Bark, Pinecone) • Foam tape • PVA glue

INSTRUCTIONS:
Cut out Trading Card. Ink edges with Bark. • Attach 2 eyelets between the Date and Artist lines. Insert metal ends of elastic closure through the eyelets. • Cover chipboard card with Red scrapbook paper. Ink edges with Pinecone.• Stamp heart on Khaki folder with Perfect Medium. Brush on Perfect Pearls. Brush off excess. • Cut out 'live', 'laugh' and 'love'. Ink with Pinecone. Glue to file folders. • Trim photos. Adhere inside folders. • Glue Black folder to covered chipboard. Attach brass flashpoint above Black file with brad. Glue Red and Khaki folders over Black file. • Apply foam tape to edges of chipboard back. Attach chipboard piece to Artist Trading Card back.• Wrap elastic around front of folders.

CIRCUS PATTERN
(fold on dotted line)

Making your Own Envelopes

1. Cut a square of stiff cardstock.

2. Trace it onto chipboard.

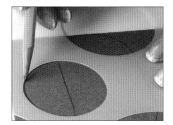

3. Using a circle template, draw a scallop on each side of the square.

What a Circus!

I love double-sided cardstock. You get two sides for the price of one! It's especially great to use for envelopes where both sides will show.

MATERIALS:
Circus cardstock • Mosaic Tiles paper • Cutable strips: Toy Blocks, Ransom Letters • Red metal clip • 2½" x 3½" chipboard card • Metal letters • Red eyelet • Joker charm • Jump ring • Colored plastic confetti • *Tsukineko* Bark Versacolor cube • PVA glue

INSTRUCTIONS:
Cover chipboard card with Mosaic paper. Trim. Ink with Bark. • Cut out letters and tickets. Ink edges. Trace the template onto two-sided Circus cardstock and cut out. Score and fold envelope flaps with Yellow side facing out. Ink edges. Set an eyelet in the top flap. Attach joker charm. • Glue tickets and confetti inside envelope. Glue envelope to card. Fold flaps of envelope closed. Glue "Circus" metal letters in place. • Attach clip.

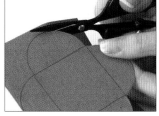

4. Cut out your template.

Beautiful Dreamer

This hinge technique works anytime you want two cards bound together so they open.

MATERIALS:
Exotic Lands Trading Cards • Dark Words Cutable strip • Library cardstock • Mosaic Tiles paper • 2½" x 3½" chipboard card • Indian coin • Postage stamps • Brass hinge • 3 spiral clips • 4 brass bells • Rubber stamps (*Just Rite* word; *Tin Can Mail* Cancellation) • *Tsukineko* inks (Black Impress; Bark Versacolor cube) • Fibers • PVA glue • Glue stick

INSTRUCTIONS:
Top card: Cut out Trading Card. Ink edges with Bark. Stamp "Beautiful Dreamer" in Black. • Trace card onto Library cardstock and adhere to card with solid side facing out. • Punch a hole on the right side and thread fibers through. Attach bells to fiber ends. On back side, adhere postage stamps and stamp with cancellation stamp. • **Bottom card**: Lay chipboard over Mosaic Tiles paper and trace twice. Cut out and bond to both sides of chipboard card with glue stick. Adhere coin with PVA glue. • Cut out words. Age with Bark ink. Adhere with PVA glue. • Put spiral clips on 3 sides. • Connect front and back covers with Brass hinge.

Standing Photo Frame

This is a great idea for a miniature photo frame. The hinge is stiff enough that when opened, the ATC makes its own little stand.

MATERIALS:
Cutable strips: Dark Words, Typewriter, Print Blocks, Number Blocks • Cardstock: Print Blocks, Rulers • Slide Mounts & Tags: Rulers; Books • Metal hinge • 2½" x 3½" chipboard card • Small photo • *Tsukineko* Versacolor cubes (Bark, Old Rose) • PVA glue • Glue stick

INSTRUCTIONS:
Card: Cut out Red section of Dark Words Cutable strip. Glue to the Print Blocks paper so the solid side shows. Trim. Ink edges with Old Rose. • **Flap**: Glue Ruler slide mount to the solid side of Ruler cardstock so the rulers show. Trim. Age edges with Bark ink. • Glue photo to small Books tag and insert tag into mount. • **Hinge shim**: Trace top part of hinge onto chipboard. Cut out. Place under top part of hinge to equalize the height. Adhere shim to hinge with PVA glue. • **Finish**: Attach hinged mount to card with brads. • Cut out elements for inside message. Age with Bark ink. Glue to card under the flap.

Memories of Europe

If you have never traveled, make this card about a place you have always wanted to visit.

MATERIALS:
Traveler cardstock • Mail Art Backs Trading Card • Cutable strips: Letter Squares, Typewriter, Pastel Words • Black mini file folder • Compass charm • Rose fiber • Gold closure piece • Travel ephemera • *Tsukineko* Bark Versacolor Cube • *Ranger* Latte Adirondack alcohol ink • PVA glue • Glue stick

INSTRUCTIONS:
Cut out trading card. Adhere a small piece of scrap paper to top left corner of card back. • Adhere Traveler cardstock, leaving a small corner turned down in top left corner to expose scrap paper. Age edges with Bark ink. • Cut out words and letters. Age all with Bark ink. Glue in place with PVA. • Insert travel ephemera into folder. Tie Rose fiber to closure piece. Glue fiber ends to back side of folder with PVA. • Adhere folder to card at an angle. • Apply Latte ink directly to compass charm to age. Adhere charm to top left corner.

Using Perfect Pearls

1. Stamp heart stamp on Khaki folder with Perfect Medium.

2. Brush gently with one or more colors Perfect Pearls.

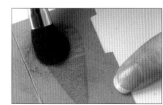

3. Brush off excess around image.

Travel, Explore

Explore the possibilities of mosaic art with this beginner project.

MATERIALS:

Letter Squares Cutable strip • Black metal clip • Life's Journey Stamp Collage paper • Burgundy paper • Black cardstock • 2½" x 3½" chipboard card • *Tsukineko* Versacolor cubes (Bark, Pinecone) • PVA glue

INSTRUCTIONS:

Cover chipboard card with Burgundy paper. Edge with Bark ink. • Trim postage stamp from Life's Journey paper. Adhere to chipboard scrap. Cut in ½" diagonal cuts. • Cut Black cardstock 1⅝" x 1⅞". Adhere to chipboard scrap. Adhere mosaic pieces to Black cardstock. • Adhere mosaic to card. • Cut out "Travel" and "Explore" words. Edge with Pinecone ink. Adhere to card. Add clip.

Queen of Hearts

Trading cards offer the opportunity to experiment with a variety of art forms on a small scale. Create a regal mosaic with this simple-to-make Queen of Hearts card.

MATERIALS:

Jack, Queen, King Trading Cards • Red wire clip • Crown charm • 2½" x 3½" chipboard card • 4 Red rhinestones • Black acrylic paint • *Tsukineko* Bark Versacolor cube • PVA glue • Foam tape

INSTRUCTIONS:

Paint chipboard card with Black acrylic paint. Let dry. • Trim Queen card down to edge of Qs. Cut randomly into pieces. Adhere pieces to Black chipboard using PVA glue starting with top edge. Once the top row of pieces is adhered with even spaces between the pieces, arrange the left side and glue. • Add four Red rhinestones over small hearts. • Add crown charm in the center with foam tape. Attach clip.

Good Fortune

Here's a fun and inexpensive piece you can create from leftover paper scraps. I learned it from the very talented Mary Jo McGraw. I keep a cigar box full of scraps that I can use for this type of mosaic. You can create all kinds of shapes; however, I chose an Asian coin for this card to symbolize Good Fortune.

MOSAIC PATTERNS

MATERIALS:

Blue wire clip • 2½" x 3½" Black cardstock for card • 2" x 4" Chipboard • Paper scraps • Gold leaf pen • *Tsukineko* ('love' metal stamp; Encore Gold Metallic ink) • Punches (2" circle, Corner rounder, ½" square) • *Bunch of Fun* Chinese alphabet rubber stamps • *JudiKins* (Diamond Glaze, Mizuhiki cord) • Red liner tape (in sheet form or very wide roll) • Foam tape

INSTRUCTIONS:

Card: Round corners on Black card. Stamp 'Good Fortune' on bottom of card. Edge card in Gold ink. Let dry. • **Paper piecing**: Cover 2" x 4" chipboard with red liner tape. Peel protective cover off tape. Cut scrap paper in narrow strips from ⅛" to ¼" in width. Cut pieces of mizuhiki cord into 4" lengths. Lay several strips of paper over taped chipboard followed by a piece of mizuhiki cord. Repeat until the chipboard is covered. Cut into ¼" wide strips. • **Coin mosaic**: Punch a 2" circle of Black cardstock with a square punch in the middle of the circle so that it resembles an Asian coin. • Position on card and stamp an Asian symbol through the hole. • Cover the circle with red liner tape, trimming the tape from the center square. Remove protective layer of tape. Lay strips over coin, leaving the center hole bare. Trim excess around coin. Edge with Gold leaf pen. Cover with Diamond Glaze. Adhere to card with foam tape. • Add clip.

Love Token

Have you thought of cutting up a sticker to make a mosaic? Adhering the sticker to chipboard makes the pieces easy to handle. This is a must-try idea.

MATERIALS:

Valentine Stickers • Two 2½" x 3½" chipboard cards • Black cardstock • Gold metallic pen • PVA glue

INSTRUCTIONS:

Cover chipboard card with Black cardstock. • Adhere sticker to the other chipboard card. Trim to 2" x 3". Cut sticker into tiles ½" square. Arrange on Black cardstock with a slight border on both sides and glue in place with PVA glue. • Using a metallic pen, add a thin line of Gold down each side.

Making a Mosaic

1. Adhere paper strips and cord to chipboard with red liner tape.

2. Cut into strips.

3. Punch a 2" circle. Punch out a square in the center.

4. Cover with red liner tape.

5. Adhere mosaic strips and cord onto coin.

6. Edge with Gold and cover with Diamond Glaze.

Mosaics

Mosaics are an easy way to turn the ordinary into the extraordinary. Just remember that the piece of art you cut into mosaic pieces must be smaller than the piece to which you adhere it, allowing room for the spaces. Also remember, the more pieces you cut, the more challenging it will be to achieve a balanced appearance in the finished piece.

Windows and Doors

I love ATCs that have interactive parts. These cards all have panels that open and close to reveal little surprises inside.

School Daze

Personalize your ATC with school photos. They're the perfect size for sharing.

MATERIALS:

Library cardstock • Cutable strips: Typewriter, Letter Squares • Photo • Negative strip • Traveler Tape • Brass brad • Bronze metallic thread • 2½" x 3½" chipboard card • *Tsukineko* Bark Versacolor cube • PVA glue • Double-sided tape • Glue dots

INSTRUCTIONS:

Center chipboard card over spelling book on Library cardstock and trace. Cut out. • Cut a door according to template. Insert brad for door knob. • Cut four 6" strands of Bronze thread. Wrap threads over knob and tie. Trim as desired. • Cut out letters. Age with Bark ink. Glue in place. • Slide photo into negative sleeve. Center negative inside door area and trace on chipboard card. Cut four lengths of Traveler Tape and stick each one around the edge of the tracing. • Adhere the photo with glue dots to the chipboard card. Adhere spelling book cover with PVA glue.

SCHOOL DAZE
PATTERN

Making a Tape Transfer

1. Lay tape over desired image and burnish.

2. Soak for 5 minutes.

The Thought of You Sings

Tape transfer allows you to create some lovely effects. This Eiffel Tower transfer is just one example.

MATERIALS:

Pastel Words Cutable strip • Postale cardstock • Clear tape • 2 Teal brads • *Raindrops on Roses* "The Thought of You" rubber stamp • *Tsukineko* inks (Black Impress, Teal StazOn) • PVA glue • Glue stick

INSTRUCTIONS:

Trim Blue words card from Cutable strip. Trace onto child's photo on Postale cardstock. Trim. Glue to Blue words card. • Trace card onto writing on bottom left of Postale and cut out. Make a cathedral cutout using template. • Lay tape onto Eiffel Tower image. Burnish well with bone folder. Soak in water for 5 minutes. Gently rub paper off back of tape. Adhere tape to front center of window with glue stick and trim. • Re-cut window. Edge window opening and card gently with Teal ink. • Stamp "The thought of you sings" on both sides of tape transfer with Black ink. • Affix Teal brads to window. Glue window to card with PVA.

3. Gently rub backing off tape.

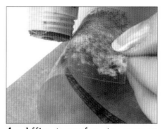

4. Affix transfer to paper using glue stick.

EIFFEL TOWER
PATTERN

Keys to My Heart

What's behind door number 2? Whatever your heart desires! Put your lucky numbers on the front of this door card.

MATERIALS:
Valentine stickers • Bingo cardstock • 4 Copper heart brads • 2 Black flashpoints • 2½" x 3½" chipboard card • 2 Copper keys • Copper metallic thread • *Ranger* inks (Tea Dye Distress, Latte Adirondack alcohol) • *Tsukineko* (Black Impress ink, Bark Versacolor cube) • PVA glue • Glue stick

INSTRUCTIONS:
Lay the chipboard card over the Bingo cardstock and trace it 3 times. Two of the cards will be used on the Red side and one on the numbered side. Cut out all three. • Sandwich chipboard between 2 Red pieces of cardstock. Adhere with glue stick. • Cut and score third sheet of cardstock using the double-door template. • Attach flashpoints with heart brads and add 2 more brads for door knobs. • Age keys with Latte ink. Thread onto Copper thread. Attach to brads. • Put Valentine stickers centered on Red cardstock covered chipboard. Adhere bingo cover to sticker card using PVA glue. • Decorate back of card as desired.

KEYS TO MY HEART PATTERN

Don't Worry, Be Happy

You will put on a happy face every time you open the windows of this fun card.

MATERIALS:
Rulers cardstock • Cutable strips: Print Blocks, Typewriter, Toy Blocks, Letter Squares, Wings & Things • Tan cardstock • 2½" x 3½" chipboard card • Tan fiber • 2 Black eyelets • *JudiKins* Print background stamp • *Tsukineko* inks (Versamark, Bark Versacolor) • Circle punches (⅛", ½") • PVA glue • Glue stick

INSTRUCTIONS:
Stamp Print background on Tan cardstock using Versamark ink. • Cut an opening in the card using the template provided. • **Closure:** Adhere a scrap of Rulers cardstock onto chipboard using a glue stick. Punch a ⅛" hole in the cardstock and then a ½" hole around that. Repeat. Ink the edges with Bark. Punch a ⅛" hole in either side of the opening on the Tan card. Attach one of the circles using an eyelet. Drop a fiber through the other hole in the Tan cardstock and then set the other eyelet so that the fiber is caught between the circle and the Tan cardstock. This fiber will loop around the other circle to make the closure. • **Finish:** Cut out the letters "Don't worry". Age with Bark ink. Glue to card with PVA. • Glue the chipboard card to the Rulers side of the cardstock so that the Dark Brown side shows. Adhere Tan window to that card. Cut out the letters "Be happy" and baby image. Ink with Bark. Glue in place.

DON'T WORRY PATTERN

Making a Window Closure

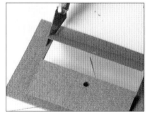

1. Cut an opening according to the template.

2. Punch ⅛" holes out of Rulers cardstock that has been bonded to chipboard.

3. Punch ½" circles around the ⅛" holes to make reinforcements.

4. Loop a fiber through one hole.

5. Attach reinforcement with an eyelet.

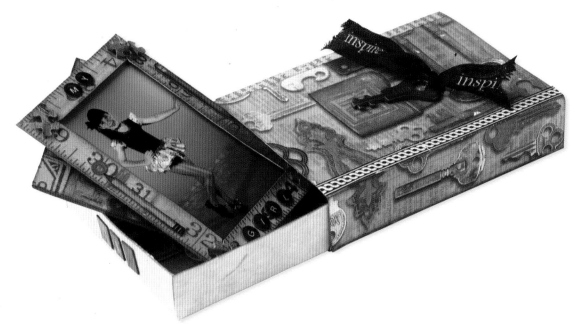

ATC Matchbox

Here's a great pattern to make your own matchbox for storing ATCs. Whether you're hosting a swap or just trying to organize your collection, it's an easy project to make. I suggest copying this pattern and tracing it onto chipboard for quick and easy use. Make notches where the score lines are. Then you can easily line up a ruler to make scoring a snap. I love using double-sided cardstock for this project since it eliminates the need to line the box. A single piece will make one matchbox.

MATERIALS:
Lock and Key cardstock • Print Blocks Cutable strip • Antique key • Black ribbon • Traveler Tape • *Tsukineko* Pinecone Versacolor cube • PVA glue

INSTRUCTIONS:
Trace pattern on plain side of cardstock. Cut out. Punch holes. Score on dashed lines. • **Bottom**: Apply PVA glue to flap A. Fold sides B up and the tabs in, to the center of the box. Fold the end flaps A over the tabs and adhere it to the tabs. • Cut out ATC letters. Ink the edges with Pinecone. Adhere with PVA glue to end of box. • **Sleeve**: Fold all score marks to form a box shape. Apply glue to the end tab C and adhere it to D. • Ink all edges with Pinecone. • Apply a piece of Traveler Tape to each side of the top of box. • Thread ribbon through holes. Tie key onto box with ribbon, leaving it to dangle. • Insert bottom of box into sleeve.

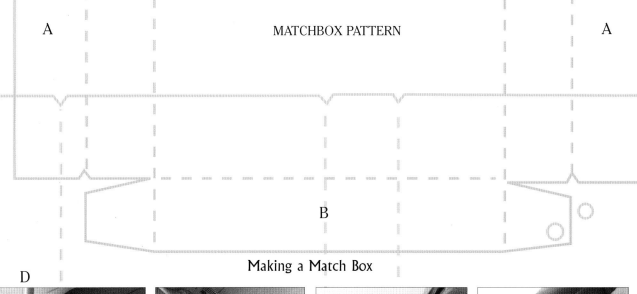

A   MATCHBOX PATTERN   A

B

B

D

Making a Match Box

1. Trace pattern from chipboard to light side of double-sided cardstock.

2. Score where indicated.

3. Cut out pieces.

4. Assemble using PVA glue.